# WALL STREET & Wildflowers

# WALL STREET & *Wildflowers*

*Choices about Life in Corporate America*

**Michael J. Vandermark, Ph.D.**

**Spirit-at-Work Publications**
**Phoenix, Arizona**

Spirit-at-Work Publications

Cover: Wall Street & Wildflowers by Donna Corwin and Russ Noble



First Edition

Printed in the United States of America

Wall Street & Wildflowers

Order from:

Spirit-at-Work Publications
1459 E. McLellan Boulevard
Phoenix, Arizona 85014

Library of Congress Catalog Card Number: 95-73086

---

1. **Library of Congress Cataloging-in-Publication Data**
2. Vandermark, Michael J.
3. Wall street & wildflowers: choices about life in corporate america
   p. cm.
   Includes index.
4. 1. Spiritual life. 2. Corporate culture. 3. Quality of work life. 4. Leadership — religious aspects. 5. Leadership — moral and ethical aspects. 6. Vocational guidance. I. Title
5. HD57.7.XX 1996
6. ISBN 0-9650390-0-5 Hardcover
7. ISBN 0-9650390-1-3 Softcover

---

FIRST EDITION

HB printing 10 9 8 7 6 5 4 3 2 1

First paperback printing January 1996

# *Dedication*

*Dedicated with full heart to:*

*My parents, Bernard and Alvara Vandermark,*
*Who have always had faith in me.*

*My sisters, Barbara, Jan, Gerri, and Toni,*
*For their patience waiting for me.*

*My children, Michael and Whitney,*
*Whom I long to know better.*

*The women who taught me love:*
*Becky, with her youth and vitality;*
*Linda, with her insight and humor;*
*Sandy, with her healing touch, courage, and warmth;*
*Susan, with her compatibility and intimacy.*

*This book could not have happened without these people*
*who have so powerfully and positively*
*affected my life.*

# *Contents*

## *Acknowledgments*

It is important that I first mention the poets who have influenced me heavily during the writing of this book. Notably, my dear friend and long time mentor, **Judy Stevens-Long**. Her creative genius strongly led to the creation of the characters Geraldine Blouch and Rhonda, as well as the inspiration needed to write "Gather Me" and "Personal Tactics 1.1.2." I am also grateful for the work of **Coleman Barks** and his magnificent translations of Rumi. Reading and listening to Coleman's work led me to understanding myself more profoundly as a spiritual being and to developing the inspiration to move forward.

I learned along my path of authorship that the actual writing of a book is sometimes the easier part of bringing it to reality. Accordingly, I owe a deep debt of gratitude to **Donna Corwin**, a highly creative and delightful person, who sat with me time after time, offering insight and feedback about my initial ideas and contemplations. With Donna's encouragement, the book grew from a few poems to a more encompassing work, one that led me to feeling far more fulfilled for writing it.

**Russ Noble**, a highly creative, warm, and humorous colleague, deserves much credit for the design and formatting of the book cover as well as the aesthetics of the book itself. If this book caught your eye, and led you to pick it up and contemplate the blending together of sunset, skyline, and wildflowers, then you were probably responding to the result of Russ's work.

I also realized as I progressed, that meticulous editing and I were not meant for one another. I was fortunate to meet and develop a meaningful relationship with **Susan Johns**, whose enthusiasm and support, as well as uncanny editing ability, were ever present during the final stages of writing. To Susan, I am also deeply indebted.

Prior to going to press, I was blessed with important and insightful evaluation and feedback from many people. Their comments led me to finalizing the manuscript and more deeply feeling the sense of purpose I first noticed when I started writing. My deepest appreciation is extended to **Dave and Judy Walker, Alison Arnold, Elizabeth Cheatham, Bob Enderle, Pam Bellmore, Elisabeth Vaillancourt, Joan Levine, Kem Metz, Dick Doughton, Vickie Sullivan, Maureen Theobald, Barb and Mark Dinunzio, Brenda Sperduti, Ron Venckus, Dr. Stefanie Spera, Katharina Von Rhau, Jeanne Schulze,** and **Dr. Pat Kerstner**.

A final, and very important acknowledgment: My deepest thanks for the guidance, learning, and feedback during my stay at the Gestalt Institute of Phoenix. To **Bob Mosby, Kat Von Rhau, Scott Hendrickson, Arnold Thaw, and Judith Geer**, a profound and heartfelt breath of love and appreciation.

# *Introduction*

Welcome dear reader. Thank you for looking at this introduction. I hope you will continue reading, this page is important.

This book is not about profitability, productivity, the bottom line, strategic plans, power, tactics, marketing strategies, how to hire the right person, quality, or other similar business topics found in Corporate America. It is not a "manager's guidebook," although managers may find certain poetry, insights, or choices helpful. So might non-managers. It is not a training manual per se, but can be used to stimulate discussion among groups. It contains no statement of recent or past organizational theory, nor any academic insights.

The book is about the positive and negative experiences of human beings working in Corporate America. It is applying the rhythm, language, and emotion of poetic verse to life in the American workplace. My intent was to capture a paradox, to put into verse the feelings, positive and negative, about being part of a system capable of incredible contribution to mankind as well as overwhelming annihilation of the human spirit.

While writing the book, I sought extensive feedback from colleagues who, like me, have devoted many years of their lives to corporate work. I wanted to know if poetry about Corporate America served a purpose, satisfied some need, or was meaningful. I listened intently and decided to move forward with the book. I knew writing the poetry was the most profound way for me to express how I feel about being a part of Corporate America, complete with its trials and tribulations.

Along the way, feedback from people reviewing the book led me to adding **Insights** and **Choices**. These are offered to the reader as an addendum to the poetry, as a way to further investigate the meaning of the poetry, and to embellish the experience of poetry with some pragmatic insights and choices. I once heard a trainer say, during the introduction of her seminar, "Take what you like and leave the rest." I offer these insights and choices in the same spirit of adult learning in which I first experienced them.

Thank you, once again, for spending time with me on this page, and special thanks if you have purchased this book. I experienced a great deal of pleasure writing it. I hope it adds to your enjoyment also.

*MJV*
*December, 1995*

# WALL STREET & *Wildflowers*

*Choices about Life in Corporate America*

**Half of the world is composed of people who have something to say and can't, and the other half who have nothing to say and keep on saying it.**

*—Robert Frost*

## The Memo

If I said what I
thought you said
he said
then what she said I said
about the memo
probably isn't what
you said
I thought I
said. Perhaps.

However, if we
look at it from
another perspective, then
what she said the memo
said was said by you
about what I said
she said about what you
said I said
then it would make what
she said relatively
true.

So, what was it that
was said? Can you say?

# The Memo

## *Insights*

The words we choose may not mean the same thing
to other people.

Fifty-five percent of a message is body language; thirty-eight
percent tone; only seven percent in words chosen . . .
no wonder memos are tricky.

Expressing feelings at work can be difficult, some people
don't want to hear how you feel.

No one knows what you want except you.

Immediate feedback leads to improvement,
that goes for all of us.

# The Memo

## *Choices*

- Write a memo about writing memos.
- Ask for feedback from peers about your communication effectiveness, your friends will tell you—honestly.
- If you trust your boss, ask for ideas or suggestions related to becoming a better communicator at work. If you don't trust your boss, ask a friend or soulmate.
- Be willing to share your thoughts about personal strengths and weaknesses on the job with those who work with you.
- Admit making mistakes, and own your shortcomings. It is difficult for all of us, yet well worth the effort.

**The maintenance and enhancement of perceived self are the motives behind all behavior.**

—*A.W. Combs*

# Elevators

Trapped.

Shy ones
  look at
    the floor.

Bold ones look
  into your
    eyes.

Don't stop now elevator.

# Elevators

## *Insights*

The American comfort zone for closeness to another person is 18 inches.

Extroverted people are energized by being with others.

Introverts are energized by being alone.

The world is full of interesting people,
most are strangers to us.

Negative thoughts about ourselves lead us to avoiding talking to strangers.

Sometimes elevators stop when you don't want them to.

# Elevators

## *Choices*

- If you want to get better at approaching others, practice making eye contact as you pass people in your workplace.
- Make it a point to smile at one or two people, watch for their reaction (especially in elevators, they're trapped too). Chances are, you'll be pleased with your effort.
- Practice the art of complete dialogue—start by asking questions about the other person, follow with listening skills that convince the other person that she or he is being listened to, and be willing to mention a few things about yourself, that is, personalize your conversation.
- Create a personal list of "icebreakers," if you need them, such as asking for directions, offering a compliment, commenting on the weather or a current event, or a statement of how you are feeling in the moment (this is scary for some)—"I'm always a little shy in elevators, are you?"

**Strange is our situation here upon earth. Each of us comes for a short visit, not knowing why, yet sometimes seeming to a divine purpose. From the standpoint of daily life, however, there is one thing we do know: That we are here for the sake of others, . . . for the countless unknown souls with whose fate we are connected by a bond of sympathy. Many times a day, I realize how much my own outer and inner life is built upon the labors of people, both living and dead, and how earnestly I must exert myself in order to give in return as much as I have received.**

*—Albert Einstein*

# Customer Service

"May I have your
attention"

"There is nothing
we can do at this
time"

"Thank You"

# Customer Service

## *Insights*

Our purpose in life is to serve others.

No customers, no money.

The customer is always right, except when
dealing with the government.

Everyone has at least one customer, or more, somewhere.
Some are internal, some aren't.

Your customers think the way you do
when you're the customer.

According to research, a strong personal relationship
with customers predicts repeat business
better than customer satisfaction.

Although it is necessary to respond to customers,
it is also important to hold to established
policies, practices, and processes for
employees to follow . . . It's a fine line.

# Customer Service

## *Choices*

- Meet with your customers, get to know them very, very well. Ask them if you are providing the service that will keep them satisfied. Ask for suggestions or ideas about how to improve your service to them or the nature of the product you create.
- Investigate ways to increase the attractiveness of your product or service to your customers.
- Facilitate a meeting designed to focus on quality issues. Is your quality effort active? Does it need updating?
- Ask existing and potential customers to meet with you as you co-design your next product or service.
- Talk to customers openly about your feelings toward them, overcome your fear to have to stay black-and-white, customers experience a full range of emotion, just like the rest of us. Connecting at the heart level with a customer is a logical thing to do.

**If you want employees to improve, let them overhear the nice things you say about them to others.**

*—Haim Ginott*

**The person who has been punished is not thereby simply less inclined to behave in a given way; at best, he learns to avoid punishment.**

*—B. F. Skinner*

# Reasons Why People Should Judge Each Other With Performance Appraisals

**THIS PAGE INTENTIONALLY LEFT BLANK**

# Reasons Why People Should Judge Each Other With Performance Appraisals

## *Insights*

Feedback is not the same as appraisal (judgment). At its best, feedback is unbiased information that is useful when making decisions.

Adults do not want to be judged by other adults, judgment annihilates intimacy.

Intimacy means having the ability to be open and honest with someone while knowing they will accept and honor what you say without judgment.

Direct, open, non-judgmental feedback from people on the receiving end of your performance is important and necessary. It builds intimacy.

Appraisal is as much a system of punishment as it is reward. If you make a mistake and your reward ($$) is withheld, that's punishment.

Punishment will change behavior, but most of the time the behavior change will be short-lived.

# Reasons Why People Should Judge Each Other With Performance Appraisals

## *Choices*

- We change by allowing ourselves to become who we are, not by trying to be someone we aren't (the paradoxical theory of change—Fritz Perls). Devote time to outside counseling, if need be, to discover your purpose in life. Who are you? Why are you here? That is, what are you supposed to be doing?

- Identify components of your job that underutilize your talent. Develop a plan to contribute more to your job by using the talents you have. Once you are clear about ways to better utilize your talents, discuss your desires with your boss if you are comfortable in so doing. If you are not comfortable approaching your boss, your relationship with her or him is probably a more pressing issue to deal with.

- Decide upon a way to get feedback related to your performance. Options include your boss, your boss's boss, a natural mentor, friends, associates, customers, peers, and of course, yourself.

- As you get feedback, take notes, decide if and when you are going to make any changes. To do nothing is to make the decision to remain in the same situation.

**When you know what your values are, making decisions becomes easier.**

*—Glenn Van Ekeren*

# Laptop Lessons

If I had only
five years to live,
I wouldn't save money on
transportation expenses, or make people
feel bad when they made a mistake.
I would support the management fad
of the month just for
the hell of it, and
tell more jokes in meetings.

If I had only
four more years to live,
I wouldn't worry about
performance evaluations,
about judgment, about
criticality. I would
wear make-you-laugh ties and
funny socks. I would breathe
in your laughter and spirit,
cry your tears with you,
and always cherish your friendship.

If I had only
three more years to live,
job security would finally be understood,

my presentations would come from
my intuitive heart,
I would throw away my calculator,
and start campfires with the
Wall Street Journal.

If I had only
            two more years to live,
            I would show pictures of my family
to cafeteria workers, make friends with
taxi drivers, fall in love
            with my co-workers, laugh with
            the consultants,
and always remember to plug in my
laptop computer.

If I had only
            one more year to live,
            I would tell my secrets to
everyone, spend money on expensive briefcases,
look less busy, not worry about
            my pay grade range, and
take long, long vacations.

If I had only
            six months to live,
            I would find another

job just for fun, learn people's names,
walk in the park more often,
        write my life story,
        absolutely refuse to worry,
and take a mortician to lunch.

If I had only
        one month to live,
        I would look out the window
more often, spend quiet time just <u>being</u>,
drink fancy coffees while I
        drive, and laugh at a 30% raise.

If I had only
        one week to live
        I would find new meaning in
water fountains, look more closely
        into your eyes,
        give my final stand-up presentation,
and make love after hours on the staff
conference table.

When I have only
        one hour to live,

I will embrace a
new mission and vision, truly
understand values, not worry
too much about goals,
and celebrate the wonder and awe of
my life's largest paradigm shift.

But,
batteries (and life) being
what they are,
I would still plug in my
laptop computer.

# Laptop Lessons

## *Insights*

We all let others know what our values are.

We do it by striving for certain goals whether professional or personal, by the vows we take or avoid, by the nature of our relationships, what we own, friendships we invest in, churches we attend, movies we see, and so on.

Well-developed values at work will serve you well during the tough times as well as the good times.

Practicing what you preach is a way of holding to your values.

Being able to live out your values in your workplace is one of life's most precious gifts.

# Laptop Lessons

## *Choices*

- Have a discussion with a person you trust about what values speak most powerfully to you. Take notes, refer to them occasionally. Listen to what the other person says about his or her values. Discuss the differences.
- Recall times when you have made tough decisions that caused you to examine your personal values. Are you still holding to those values now? Why? Or why not?
- What is the greatest accomplishment of your life? What values did you hold to in order to reach your goal?
- What will be said about you when you die? Write your own eulogy, discuss it with someone close to you.
- What is your personal philosophy about life? That is, why, in your opinion, are you here? What will happen to you after you die? Where were you before you were born?

**Someday after we have mastered the air, the winds, the tides, and gravity, we will harness for God the energies of love. And then for the second time in the history of the world, man will have discovered fire.**

*—Teilhard de Chardin*

# It WOULD Be

Would it be
love to be
joined to
my work like
wetness
to water?

To outrun the
shadowpower of the
politicians?
To engage the
lightsource of passion
for what
I
DO?

Would it be spirit-touch
on my body
the kiss
of my life
the kiss I long for
the kiss of my
contribution, of
knowing why I am here?

Would it be possible to

find my heart in
Corporate America

to find a work-secret
whispered softly
feather soft?
whispered?

Felt?
Touched?
Embraced?

Would it be?

# It WOULD Be

## *Insights*

There is a huge difference between a job and a calling.

A job often leads to clock-watching. A calling in life or passion for work means doing something we love so much, it becomes timeless.

Each of us has the ability to discover our calling.

Our spirituality can be deeply felt by doing work we love. Our work becomes part of our spiritual journey.

Our work should in some way, directly or indirectly, serve our community.

# It WOULD Be

## *Choices*

- Read *Artful Work: Awakening Joy, Meaning, and Commitment in the Workplace* by Dick Richards.
- Also, read *The Seven Spiritual Laws of Success* by Dr. Deepak Chopra.
- If reading doesn't work for you, but you are still interested in finding meaningful work in Corporate America, contact a career counselor, one who consults from the heart as well as the head.
- Browse through the career development literature in your favorite bookstores. You'll be surprised what is available.
- Daydream that you've been given the opportunity to do any work you want with all requirements about education or experience removed. What work would you do? After you identify it, find someone who is doing it and interview them thoroughly.

**Most people believe they see the world as it is. However, we really see the world as we are.**

—*Anonymous*

# Tips on the Organizational Life From Geraldine Blouch

Listen, here's the way to survive at work; everybody kisses up to the boss at performance review time. The human resources people think you know the answers, your boss will find out if you interview for another job, typos piss people off, no one knows if your underwear is clean or dirty, two hours after the meeting no one remembers if you were late or not, don't believe everything. It's physically impossible to poke your eye out with a stick, memos are someone else's reality, if your boss makes a play at you, it's worth it to tell the press, save off-color jokes for people you trust, newspapers make bathrooms more enjoyable. If you meet someone in the office, but you don't want to cook breakfast, spend your night alone. Remember that the purpose of business is to keep the customer happy. If I were you I would keep track of my health benefits and always update my resume. Don't get drunk at company parties, but fantasies never hurt anyone.

# Tips on the Organizational Life From Geraldine Blouch

## *Insights*

There is no "perfect" workplace.

How can there be? There are no "perfect" human beings.

All of your experiences are a signal from deep
within yourself back to yourself. The signal
is about what your senses are perceiving in the universe.

As you see it,
so it is.

Anyone else may see it differently.

"It" can be anything experienceable in life.

Geraldine is one of those people
who derives satisfaction
from complaining.

# Tips on the Organizational Life From Geraldine Blouch

## *Choices*

- Stress accelerates the aging processes of the human body. So, if you are experiencing stress, you are physiologically getting older faster. Maintain an active stress management program.
- Pay attention to politics at work. Some people are better at schmoozing. If you aren't, recognize the fact and decide if you want to live your life in such a setting. Better to face the temporary stress of a job search than remain miserable. This is hard. Geraldine hates political BS.
- Practice self-disclosure with people you trust, it works.
- Don't be too straightforward with people who are not your allies, especially if they have power. The one with the most power stays.
- If you meet someone like Geraldine, offer her kindness and compassion. It will come back to you.

**Imagination is more important than knowledge.**

*—Albert Einstein*

**Inspiration and imagination go hand in hand.**

*—Anonymous*

# On S-I-M-P-L-I-F-I-C-A-T-I-O-N

The manual says "simplify" . . .

OK: Goodbye!

Hello life!
Let's take it
easy and call
committees of wildflowers
ocean fantasies and
long ago lovers  Let's
celebrate feelings all
feelings especially our
voice and mail it –
mail it far away to
petticoat places of
romance and manlihood

Let's frolic and fail –
fail to be
overly successful at "doing"
Let's not do
Let's simplify
Let's be
Let's just
be

# On S-I-M-P-L-I-F-I-C-A-T-I-O-N

## *Insights*

There is a saying in Eastern Philosophy—
"Do Less—Accomplish More."

Taking time to "just be" creates calmness
needed for creativity and rejuvenation.

The chances of experiencing the "good idea" that
you are waiting for increases if you calm
the turbulence in your mind caused
by the hectic day-to-day routine
in Corporate America.

Meditation, simply stated, means quieting the mind.
Many are finding the experience to be
profoundly spiritual as well.

An excess of 500 studies carried out at more than
200 universities and research institutions in over 30 countries
illustrate the profound impact of meditation on the mind,
body, behavior, and environment. It works.

# On S-I-M-P-L-I-F-I-C-A-T-I-O-N

## *Choices*

- "Just be" fifteen minutes twice a day, that is, meditate. If you don't know how, seek a teacher. See what happens.

- Other ways of dealing with the hectic routine of Corporate America include stress reduction programs and exercise of all types. Commit to a program best suited for you.

- Notice what you have learned from failing. Failing leads to knowledge and growth. Celebrate your failures as well as your successes. Have an "I blew it, look what I learned" party.

- Be spontaneous about life. If you are one that prefers events and activities planned well in advance, try proceeding on an activity without making plans, just once. See if you like it.

- Go play—right now.

**The grapevine tends to exert some influence in the organization, whether for good or evil; thus an understanding of the grapevine and how it can contribute positively to the organization is important.**

*—R. Wayne Pace*
*—Don F. Fowles*

# Grapevine Devastation

76 stories involving
14 people – discussed
in hallways, bathrooms
parking lots and
during phone calls

Affairs: real or imagined, 7; trust
issues, 4; promotions and
layoffs, 9; marital problems, 21; bosses
style, 67; I'm-ready-to-quit
stories, 12.

Men:
without proper manners
without political savvy
poor listener
too much of a loner
not taking time to smell the roses
making passes at women
too rigid; over-organized
trying too hard to be liked
clueless about feelings
out of touch with reality
no patience
lousy communicator
is having an affair with so-and-so

Women:
without proper manners
without political savvy
self-help junkie
too talkative for own good
is having an affair with so-and-so
seeking status
deflects real issue with humor
overly concerned about making everyone happy
talks too much
doesn't say enough
tries to please everyone
walks all over people's feelings

Teams with internal conflict Poor meetings Lousy presentations Stupid policies Smokers Office parties Performance evaluations Clothes Hairstyles Money Love Sex

Grapevine pain
hurts most
if your
best friend
believes it.

# Grapevine Devastation

## *Insights*

According to research, nearly 75 to 90% of grapevine details are accurate.

The grapevine is one of the fastest ways to move information.

The earlier someone hears about a situation or event, the more likely he or she is to pass it on.

When details are missing, information is still passed on, even if inaccurate.

People who are most active in grapevine communication are the ones most interested in the subject or person being talked about.

# Grapevine Devastation

## *Choices*

- Be your own witness to your behavior, that is, notice how you participate in the grapevine. Do you carry the information forward? Does it stop with you?
- Decide whether your activity in the grapevine serves you well or not.
- If possible (this is hard), hold off judgment of others as they choose the way they want to respond to grapevine activity. You will be greatly appreciated for non-judgment, and you will have a less turbulent mind.
- Give yourself a self-esteem checkup if you discover that you've been wounded by the grapevine. It is natural to feel the pain of ridicule, rumor, or rejection. Seek a friend or counselor for help if you begin to feel overwhelmed.

**We go to services and read prescribed words, not to find God but to find a congregation, to find other people who are in search of the same divine presence as we are. By coming together, reading the same words together, we overcome the isolation and solitude with which each of us ordinarily lives. We all become one and we create the moment in which God is present.**

—*Rabbi Harold Kushner*

# Language

Memos Meetings Voice mail E-mail Strategic plans Team discussions Hallway gossip Flirtations Water fountain tales Grapevines Teleconferencing Proposals Videotapes Weekend retreats Responses Letters Notes Signs Bulletin boards Policies Annual reports Progress evaluations Legal advice Faxes Procedures Invitations Training manuals Thank you notes

We cannot
touch with language
the one who lives
in each of us –

the
spirit of this
workplace

# Language

## *Insights*

Aldous Huxley, noted author, mentioned that across all civilizations from the beginning of time, all peoples have shared three important beliefs about life. We (all people ever having lived) have concluded that 1) some sustaining life force or higher power exists, 2) this life force or higher power is found in each and every human being, and 3) the purpose of life is to seek this higher power (God).

Language is too limiting to grasp the essence of the higher power, of God (or whatever you perceive the higher power to be), of spirituality.

To deny spirituality exists in the workplace is to say only people without spiritual substance work there.

We hesitate to talk about God and spirituality at work, yet we all agree that a "high-spirited" workforce with increased "morale" is what we need for success.

What is morale and spirit other than our own feelings of passion for work, love of one another, joys of success, and the feeling of commitment to serving a higher purpose?

Work is spiritual, it's why we are here.

# Language

## *Choices*

- Decide if you are happy with the attention you are paying to your spiritual journey. Find a guide if you believe you need one.
- Browse a bookstore for books and audiotapes related to the type of spiritual development most meaningful to you.
- If morale is poor where you work, begin a discussion about it, seek others' input. Gather enough information to make a case for improving the spirit of your workplace. You will be surprised how much support you will receive.
- Recommit to your present position in your workplace, or, if the thought of recommitment is unappealing, think seriously about leaving. If your job simply "isn't you," find out what your calling is and seek it . . . now.
- If prayer has been missing from your life, consider revisiting it. There is amazing medical evidence that prayer affects recovering patients. If it works for them, it will work for you.

**There is no crisis to which academics will not respond with a seminar.**

—*Anonymous*

# Training Classes

Trainers eat garlic
at lunch, but
    strive to be
    rainmakers. They
talk in uninterrupted blocks,
stick to the
    objective, develop
    bottom-line consequences, and
always make proper
introductions.

Language is their tool
    they say "strategic," "quality,"
    "team," and "results"
as if they were jokes, not
dreams and audience thoughts.

Women trainers fantasize, men
    tell lies, have you noticed,
    but all trainers always know
how you perform, if
    you're honest, and if you
want to do better the next time.

Trainers say "OK" a lot
and like nuns who
    run hospitals, always have to
                                        have the last word.

# Training Classes

## *Insights*

Sometimes trainers know what they are talking about, sometimes they don't, sad but true.

Research strongly indicates that Corporate America spends millions on training that leads to literally NO behavior change.

People remember 10% of what they read, 90% of what they say and do. This statistic says a lot for developmental activities as an alternative to classroom training, at least in some cases.

Most training is conducted in the same classroom format you experienced in grammar school. Adults normally do not enjoy learning in that type of setting.

Keep 'em busy formats, simulations, and games connected to real organizational problems seem to work best and get the highest marks from participants.

# Training Classes

## *Choices*

- Invest time and effort when filling out end-of-course critiques. Good instructors respond to quality feedback.

- Don't allow the trainer to always have the last word. Say what is on your mind, you are probably correct, unless the trainer is a nun running a hospital.

- If you are in training and the course trainer is not connecting the material to everyday real-life problems, ask for (emphatically) an explanation. Your time is valuable. A good trainer will be impressed by your request and interest.

- If you have never taught a class, consider it. However (and this is important), be sure you receive the train-the-trainer education you need to be good at it. You will be far more successful and fulfilled. Mentors are also lifesavers when it comes to learning how to teach adults in Corporate America.

- Take a trainer to lunch sometime. Excellent corporate educators truly have a lot to offer. You will learn much.

**To be humble to superiors is a duty, to equals courtesy, to inferiors nobleness.**

*—Benjamin Franklin*

## Earthbound

I did not know
that in this workplace
lurked disparate
death:

that who I know, and
games I play
collide with my work devotion
like a shivery wind

blowing, marching through
me, icy cold . . .
leaving me fragile,
unwilling.

When I was younger
and quicker, I longed
to lead, to run
a course, to

direct those lesser. Aching,
my will was
for command,
control . . . domination.

All day long egothoughts

nailed me to deeds,
to **doing**, not
to **being**, but to

engagements of self, a
constant mingling of
"show and tell" like
my need

to be honored,
to be loved,
to be
the light of the moon.

Now, something in my chest
moves, sleepy, mostly . . .
I notice people
want to be happy.

Why feed them my pain?
Perhaps I should untie their
wings, be free and easy, rid
my soul of envy. If I did,

Would I then
come down
to earth?

# Earthbound

## *Insights*

Everyone has a boss. Sometimes it is your customer.

Clearly, managing is a head & heart issue. Highly successful managers understand how to balance the two.

Characteristics such as assertiveness, aggressiveness, boldness, achievement need, and dominance are found among many managers. These are deep-set personality characteristics and are highly resistant to change.

The desire to control others is **always** driven by fear of some kind, whether you are conscious of your fear or not.

Corporate politics is gamesmanship. Some players are better than you, some are not.

Power is like love . . . paradoxical . . . the more you give away, the more you receive in return.

We are human **beings**, not human **doings**. What's it like to **DO** at work? What's it like to **BE** at work? **Being** is where the spirit is.

# Earthbound

## Choices

- Browse through the increasing literature on spirituality at work. It's in the bookstores in the business section.
- Call a meeting and talk openly about the spirituality of management. Many will attend, if for no other reason than curiosity. Solicit people's views about the nature and impact of spirituality in your workplace. Use poetry as a starting place.
- Talk with others about the reality of managers truly empowering employees. Is it just a management fad, or does it work? Why would a manager want to give power away? It took years to get it.
- Urge people you work with to conduct rituals and ceremonies related to working together. Celebrate victories and losses. Develop a history together. Tell stories about how your company has come to be what it is; have parties, celebrations, outings.
- Seek feedback regarding your listening skills. Ask others if they believe you are attentive and patient. Urge them to be brutally honest. If the feedback suggests it, find a communications coach.

**What one sees depends upon where one sits.**

*—James R. Schlesinger*

# Strained Relationships at Work

Screaming, your penetrating voice rattles
my understanding of your message
and passes through me like electric current,
stymieing me, stalling me. Out of control, your
abusive hands, taken with your anger-ridden
breath in my face, create a surge in me,
a desire to shut down, to turn off,
to protect myself, to be cautious.

You seem to lose control so easily with me,
yet my inner being is continually set in motion
to please you. I feel so unnoticed,
so unappreciated, so tired.

Deeply I long for you to understand me,
to touch me gently, to honor our limited time
together. We have so much to offer each other,
the interplay of ourselves opens timeless
creativity, unbounded enjoyment,
just being together, just being . . .

We can work this out, can't we? I want to
be your partner, your companion, to feel
your gentle touch, to be the light of
your life. I'm here for you. It's your choice.

Sincerely . . . Your loyal computer

# Strained Relationships at Work

## *Insights*

Computers are now 8000 times more powerful than they were in 1950.

Most people will tell you automation is here to stay.

When we feel frustration, it is because we are being blocked from achieving a goal.

Everyone in Corporate America has devastating computer stories.

Ninety-nine (plus) percent of the time you are using it, the computer is doing <u>exactly</u> what it is supposed to do, that is, respond to what you are asking it to do.

It is impossible to keep up with all the advances in business related software.

# Strained Relationships at Work

## *Choices*

- Ask some people who work with you to rate your patience on a scale from 1 to 10. Honor their feedback, decide if it is meaningful enough to act on.
- Delve deeply into the software you use in your workplace. Chances are, you can increase your productivity and be less frustrated at the same time.
- Ask the people you know who are highly computer literate to update you regarding the latest technology. Ask for demonstrations of newer software if it can be arranged.
- If you are not computer literate, enroll in a course or two. Many courses are available through community colleges and commercial technical training centers.
- Avoid hitting your keyboard when you are frustrated with your computer. Beat up a pillow instead.

**I have often regretted my speech, never my silence.**

*—Publilius Syrus*

# Reflections on Lying at Work

you bragged about
me, I
found out, I
bragged about
you and I
was found
out

what happened?

# Reflections on Lying at Work

## *Insights*

Creating a high profile is like bungee jumping
too close to the ground.

Lack sensitivity, derail your career.

Good news: speaking out helps others.
Bad news: speaking out helps others.

Bragging is arrogance.

Sometimes arrogance moves you up.
Sometimes it moves you out.

# Reflections on Lying at Work

## *Choices*

- List 5 reasons why you want a high profile at work.
- List 5 reasons why you don't.
- Decide what kind of profile fits you best, get it.
- Gather your courage, be quiet, be willing to listen without judgment, and ask a soulmate to talk to you about your ego.
- Just do it. Then, thank your soulmate.
- A soulmate is a person who accepts you for who you are without judgment, without parenting, without a need to control you.
- Soulmates make life worth living.

**Youth longs and manhood strives, but age remembers.**

*—Oliver Wendell Holmes, Jr.*

**We grow too soon old and too late smart.**

*—Pennsylvania Dutch Saying*

**You can give without loving, but you cannot love without giving.**

*—Amy Carmichael*

# Let's Pretend

Let's pretend we're eleven
and let's learn how to
kiss, you know, like
the grown ups.

And let's pretend we
have a job, you know,
a place to go where we
have to drive to get to.

Let's pretend we can take
our own vacations and
play on the beach and
walk. I'll even hold your
hand . . . maybe.

Let's pretend we make
a lot of money so we can
buy toys 'n stuff and I'll
even let you come over and
share mine.

Let's pretend that we really
love our work, that we are

strategic in our thinking, that
quality always comes
first, that market penetration is

a business imperative, that
the cost of capital is
manageable, and that
multinational firms
understand the meaning of
love.

Let's pretend.

# Let's Pretend

## *Insights*

When you have been "talking to yourself" throughout
your life, your inner child is often the "self"
you have been talking to.

Young children know how to pretend. It is part of playing.

Many people in Corporate America don't play.

Pretending and creativity are synonymous.
Creativity is what Corporate America pays
big bucks for.

Paradox: Corporate America doesn't ask
its members to play or pretend.
It asks its members to be adults.

Playful adults create.

# Let's Pretend

## *Choices*

- Be playful at work. Bring fun gifts for people, they won't forget the gifts, or you.
- A smile is a gift, give yours away.
- Take time today to tell a close friend at your workplace how you feel about the enjoyment of working together.
- In a group, use pretending to imagine your workplace the way you would like it to be, especially regarding effectiveness and efficiency, clarity of roles, sharing of power, celebrations and rituals, customer service, and so on. Also, pretend what your workplace would be like if it were happy and joyous.
- First pretend, then act on your vision.

**When you work you are a flute**
**through whose heart the whispering of**
**the hours turns to music.**
**. . . . And what is it to work with love?**
**It is to weave the cloth with threads**
**drawn from your heart, even as if your**
**beloved were to wear that cloth.**

*—Kahil Gibran*

# Office History

In this old office
the business has fallen away
My heart is in loss
Spirit, enter, or let me leave

# Office History

## *Insights*

Some thing, some body, some entity greater than yourself influences your workplace . . . big time.

Spirit cannot be located in time and space.

If you laugh while at work, where in your body does the laughter originate? "The mind" is the wrong answer.

At the spiritual level, planning, organizing, staffing, directing, and controlling are all transcended. So are paychecks.

**Hidden** feelings of grief and loss are abundant in Corporate America.

"Gut feel" and "intuition" are acceptable terms at work. They both mean the same thing. They both mean following the heart, the spirit.

# Office History

## *Choices*

- If it is over, know it is over, accept it. Be in your grief. It is all a part of being human. Crying is healthy, do it.
- Be quiet and patient during times of loss and grief. Develop an intimate kinship with these emotions. Becoming familiar with them will serve your heart well in the future.
- Your sadness will pass as something new enters your heart. Pay attention to the change. Be alone and keep a journal about your experience.
- Be courageous in the face of the strange and unexplainable.
- Stay in contact with your Higher Power. It's probably good for business.

**Two managers were talking:**
**"Let's cut the staff meeting today."**
**"We can't. I need the sleep."**

*—Joe Griffith*

**For every minute you remain angry, you give up sixty seconds of peace of mind.**

*—Ralph Waldo Emerson*

# Poetry at the Office

Mary had a little lamb
whose fleece was white as snow
and everywhere that Mary went
she
was late!

The meeting
starts at 9:00 sharp!
Be there on time – Damn it!

# Poetry at the Office

## *Insights*

Life in Corporate America is mostly about
controlling human beings.

Some people will be nourishing to you, others toxic.

Toxic people nourish their needs to your
detriment, nourishing people find meaning and
gratification being with you.

About half of the U.S. population lives
"by the clock." Nearly 80% of those are found
in Corporate America.

Everyone has an agenda. Everyone.

# Poetry at the Office

## *Choices*

- Use a calendar. Be on time. Those are the rules. Period.
- If you don't like the rules, have a long talk with a friend about alternatives.
- When facing the anger, sarcasm, and/or belittlement of another, picture your arms crossed in front of your heart. Don't allow the other person's negativity to cause emotional damage. This imaginary shield technique works.
- Ignore abusers. Get up and leave. If the abuser is your boss, leave now! You will survive, your willingness to leave is proof.
- If you have been angry and/or abusive with another, cool off. Then thank the other person for their willingness to be with you during your anger. Non-abusive, fair-fighting is normal, honor your partner's willingness to participate with you. Your self-disclosure will strengthen your intimacy.

**It is luxury to be understood.**

*—Ralph Waldo Emerson*

# Pals

Guys talk guy talk at work mainly for safety
reasons or at least in some part out of longing
to connect at the level of the heart which is

logically a scary word given especially the notion
that expressing emotion is counterobjective to
criteria set in black and white rationality that

doesn't necessarily exclude women but does however
under extreme circumstances call for impeccable
ability to center one's being on the exclusivity of

heart of passion of longing of love of the yearning
for meaning in one's existence which of course isn't
really the issue when the Board is focusing on the

bottom line and productivity is low and commitment is
in the toilet and morale is hanging by a thread and
following objective quantifiable analysis all of the

above is ridiculous to consider given the logical outcome
of playing any other game but that of rationality
that is, everything is really black and white.

Logical to you?

# Pals

## *Insights*

The foreign language of Corporate America is
that of the heart.

It's not about being **all** heart
or **all** head, it's about balance.

Statistically, there are about as many "illogical"
women as there are "non-feeling" men in the workplace.

Interesting balance.

Passion and profitability correlate, but only one
is discussed in meetings.

It is natural to feel, logical to express.

# Pals

## *Choices*

- To develop your logical side:

  List all the arguments someone might use against an important good idea of yours.

  Write five different ways you could solve a problem. Write pros and cons.

  Do an "if then" simulation. Start by saying "I want XXX" or "I don't want XXX." Then say, "If I get X, then I will want Y, and then Z will happen." Repeat and continue to the (often surprising) conclusion.

- To develop your feeling side:

  Discuss a personal secret with a friend.

  Tell a story about someone you know, or a group you belong to. Use as many feeling words as you can.

- Practice the expression of your feelings. Find a strong feeling-type person to practice with.

**The secret of genius is to carry the spirit of the child into old age, which means never losing your enthusiasm.**

*—Aldous Huxley*

**Assume a virtue, if you have it not.**

*—William Shakespeare*

## On Whining

"Bring me solutions, not problems"
is a problem
when gentle clouds of
spring linger outside
my window, and
puffed cheeks of playfulness
penetrate my knowing.

"OK, fine." My father knew
all along about procedure,
process, policy, and
politics, but mother knew
about wind that whistled (not
five o'clock clocks) and
apple boughs, green green
grass, and the notion that
no one (no one!)
ever really misses
a deadline.

Ever.

# On Whining

## *Insights*

The only real deadline is spiritual.

To many, mothers seem strongly connected to their spirituality. It may have something to do with bearing children.

Procedure, process, policy, and politics serve a purpose. So do fathers.

Being playful is spiritual.

Spiritual workplaces have room for playfulness.

# On Whining

## *Choices*

- Strengthen your appreciation for nature. Go and be in it. Now.
- Develop a plan for having more play in your life. If you don't know how, find someone who has done it, learn how.
- Have a conversation with a retired person about the need for work/play balance throughout life.
- Continually prepare for your final deadline.

**Oh God, give us serenity to accept what cannot be changed, and courage to change what should be changed, and wisdom to distinguish the one from the other.**

*—Dr. Reinhold Niebuhr*

# In Change, Who Are We?

Total restructuring; this workplace
becomes ghostly

This vision, this plan
is a ghost to the past

Pale with anticipation
and fear

We are between dimensions
fleeing our own shadow

# In Change, Who Are We?

## *Insights*

Downsizing, restructuring, rightsizing, reengineering, merging, reorganizing, redeveloping . . . all mean the same thing—the feeling of loss of control over our destiny at work.

The past and future are both in your imagination.

Loss of control is about fear.

Transition is a word often used to describe the psychological effects of change, it's your way of responding emotionally to a change event.

All things are created twice . . .
first the vision (the pretending), then the changing
of the (pretended) vision into reality.

There are two types of change: "first order" and "second order." When you dream and the scenes change, that is first order; when you wake up, that is second order. Big difference.

Sometimes Corporate America keeps changing the scenes of the dream, when what really needs to happen for change to work is to wake up.

# In Change, Who Are We?

## *Choices*

- Become an active student of change. Buy a book on change, personal and/or organizational, and read it thoroughly.
- Choose a close friend at work, discuss your personal reactions to the changes occurring, see if the other person feels the same way. Honor each other's perceptions, they are your own realities.
- If you are unclear about changes in your workplace, approach your boss and ask to be updated. Good bosses tell the truth.
- If you secretly wish that nothing would change at work, know that about 50% of the general U.S. population feels the same way. With that in mind, champion some change effort.
- Try new behaviors that reflect major personal changes. Go to church. Don't go to church (if it's not meaningful), relate to God directly and personally. Try meditation, yoga, exercise, being in nature, adult learning of any type, expressing your feelings, listening more, experiencing more leisure time, **causing** conversations about spirit at work, writing poetry.

**Nine-tenths of the serious controversies which arise in life result from misunderstanding.**

*—Louis D. Brandeis*

# Memos in Spring

I have crumpled
the memo
from my in-basket

And which you
were probably hoping
I would react to

Forgive me
you were so businesslike
and so cold

# Memos in Spring

## *Insights*

Despite the expectations to do so, most of us cannot respond
unemotionally to the events of the workplace.

Being insensitive means being abrasive, intimidating,
bullheaded, trying hard to make others feel bad,
not asking or listening,
leaving a trail of damaged people.

It is one of the major reasons careers
become history.

What goes around comes around—what you reap
is what you sow . . . etc. If you hold this to be
true, people who are insensitive to you will get theirs
someday, yes? Will you feel better for it?

Millions of people in Corporate America are learning
that the "being" within us affects our success
as an organization as well as our
personal relationships at work.

# Memos in Spring

## *Choices*

- If a memo has a painful message, don't send it, visit in person. If you can't visit, call and be genuine.
- Every once in a while ask a person you would like to get to know better at work, "How are you doing?" Emphasize "doing." Be authentic, let them know your question is not a "ritual" question, and you are truly interested.
- If you are not truly interested, don't go through the motions. Better to be silent and ask yourself why you are not interested in developing closer relationships on the job.
- If your answer is "business is business" and you don't like the idea of developing relationships at work, write a plan to improve morale.
- If you've been cold and "businesslike," try warm and "businesslike."

**I don't know the key to success, but the key to failure is trying to please everybody.**

*—Bill Cosby*

# How To Influence Senior Management

Tranquilizers for breakfast, Rhonda sets out
to discover new friends in the executive offices if
she can find the courage, her clothes are wools and
cottons, and she doesn't drink or smoke cigarettes or
breathe, because that will make her better. She wants
her humor and business cards to make it to high
places, who cares, but her dead mother anyway. Sometimes
she loses track of her expenses, misses the bus and
combs her hair wrong, and doesn't return calls within
twenty-four hours. Today she needs to validate her
parking ticket and learn how to read financial statements.
Maybe tomorrow she'll be better at business letters and
develop a higher tolerance for ambiguity. And the next
day she will learn how to sleep without breathing, find
a taxi instead of a bus, fantasize about world-class
presentations, give up dancing, and learn how to fake
it being comfortable around senior level managers.

Maybe.

# How To Influence Senior Management

## *Insights*

We have all grown up in hierarchies such as families, schools, the military, churches, and of course, Corporate America.

It is easy to look for validation of self through the approval of others, especially those with power and influence.

Finding validation of self takes courage, a type different from the kind of courage expected at work.

Many people become tense and nervous around top level management.

If your **dependency** needs are strong, you will enjoy receiving approval from those above you. If your **dominance** needs are strong you will enjoy approving those beneath you.

Exaggerated dependency and dominance needs cause problems in the workplace.

# How To Influence Senior Management

## *Choices*

- Excellent senior managers respond best to people who have clearly defined values and boundaries, a well-defined purpose in life, and an attitude of intense contribution to the organization. Ask a co-worker if you fit in that category. Ask yourself the same question.
- Ask a senior level person whom you admire if he or she would be willing to be your mentor. Learn from them.
- Form a group and have the members answer these questions: How high a position do you want? Why? Suppose you don't get it? Then what?
- Make a list of those who are afraid of your power. Ask them "Why?"
- If you identify strongly with Rhonda, talk these feelings through with an appropriate person, someone you trust and whose opinion you value.

**He who fears something gives it power over him.**

*—Moorish proverb*

# Looking for a Boss

I spend my
career looking
for my boss.

My career is almost
over. I'm still
asleep, looking.

If and when I
find my boss, when
it happens,

will I get
the lost years
back?

# Looking for a Boss

## *Insights*

Your real boss is within.

Waking up is possible.

Meaning in life stems from waking up.

Looking for a career that serves others, calls upon your unique talents, and has spiritual meaning is what life is about.

Chances are, your boss in Corporate America can't help you.

# Looking for a Boss

## *Choices*

- Go within to find your boss; meditate, pray, spend time with your awareness centered on God in whatever way is meaningful to you.
- Join a spiritual development group.
- Start a spiritual development group, find a guide first.
- Openly discuss the spirituality of a meaningful career. See if others share your view.
- Read spirituality in the workplace literature such as *Spirit at Work* by Jay Conger and Associates, and *Stewardship* by Peter Block.

**Some men go through a forest and see no firewood.**

*—English proverb*

## Turnabout

I'm right, you're wrong
   If you don't believe it
      watch, I can

put you on hold for two
   minutes, not send you
      thank you notes

never offer you a cup of
   coffee, and convince
      you to work on

symptoms, not problems
   I've got the power, I'll
      use it too, I can

be sure that you don't
   own your own career, and that
      jet lag follows you wherever

you go; that you won't
   get anything accomplished in meetings
      except maybe promises

that you can't
   deliver on, and that your
      life becomes one big typo.

If you're not careful I'll

make sure you build your career
around the latest fad

that you forget the importance
of trust and loyalty, convince you
that you always know the answer

and lead you to forget what
love can make
or do

You are the manager
in you. I close my mouth
in hopes you'll open yours

# Turnabout

## *Insights*

Calculating, manipulative people don't come across as being spiritual.

Revenge is you getting back at you about the characteristics you don't like about you.

All of what you perceive in life is a mirror of yourself. What else can it be? Who is doing the perceiving?

Love is wanting satisfaction, security, and development for someone else to the same degree you want it for yourself.

Management fads come and go, love is here to stay. Which one has the highest credibility as a "strategic imperative"?

# Turnabout

## *Choices*

- Think back to things you have said to others that may have been damaging to your relationship. If you haven't done so, make amends now. If you made amends earlier, conduct a "checkup" to be sure your relationship is still OK.
- Attend an interpersonal skills development class, even if you believe your skills are fine. You can only get better.
- If you are a manager, muster the courage to receive performance feedback, using a reliable system, from not only the people who work for you, but your boss, your boss's boss, peers, colleagues, customers you work with, even your spouse or partner. If you are really brave, include your children, also.
- Complete the steps above even if you are not a manager.
- If you know someone who is experiencing life as "one big typo," offer your compassion and friendship as a metaphorical spell-checker or correction fluid. You will be dearly appreciated and it will come back to you.

**. . . Each of us is here to discover our true Self, to find out on our own that our true self is spiritual, that essentially we are spiritual beings that have taken manifestation in physical form. We're not human beings that have occasional spiritual experiences—it's the other way around: we're spiritual beings that have occasional human experiences.**

*—Deepak Chopra, M.D.*

# Reassign Me

This meaning of work rests in me
like a windsong. I sing for
meaning like a lover.

You want to break this mirror?
Take this stone. Reassign me.

# Reassign Me

## *Insights*

When it comes to experiencing love of our work, standard operating procedure is a myth.

Many SOP's annihilate creativity.

Even promotions kill spirit. How many people do you know who were excellent line workers, but when made managers, became clueless?

Some people love what they do and don't want to stop doing it. There is much to be learned from their passion.

Our work is a mirror of ourselves.
So is everything else we do, say, or act upon.

# Reassign Me

## *Choices*

- Ask your heart this question: "Is there something in Corporate America I could be doing—something better matched with who I am, than what I am currently doing?" If you feel the slightest physiological response, a little tingling, a rush of energy, a warmth in the center of your chest, a longing of sorts, then you have your answer.
- If you truly are well-matched with your work, celebrate the fact occasionally with an "I'm doing what I'm here to do" party or ritual.
- Help others in any way you can to experience the satisfaction you feel. Tell them how you came to decide upon your calling.
- When you talk to God, ask that your boss finds spiritual meaning at work.
- If you are a manager, think hard before you promote or transfer someone out of a position they love.

**At the death of his friend, A. H. Hallam, Lord Tennyson declared, "Tis better to have loved and lost than never to have loved at all."**

—*Anonymous*

# Boxes at Work

At work, friend sits by friend
they read the mysteries
of their lives to one another

They meet at the appointed times
Once a day, once a week,
five times a day is not enough

On a break, they sit in a nook and talk
Each morning, the second they meet
they open easily telling
dreams and stories and secrets

Watching and listening to the
two of them is to understand, as
it has been said, that when two beings
come together, spirituality becomes
visible

Anger doesn't have a chance
between these two, they respond
to each other continually while the
supervisor walks. Each knowing the

unknowing of each other, becoming the
timelessness of each other's work

> **"Your position has been eliminated. Please return after five o'clock to pick up your belongings"**

There is no early or late for us, the only way
to measure love of work is by the grandeur of the
beloved, there with us . . .
Now gone.

# Boxes at Work

## *Insights*

Being laid off is paradoxical, that is, the bad news is the good news, out of pain and chaos comes growth . . . always.

Sharing common goals, being a part of the same department, having the same boss, being in the same corporate culture—all of these contribute to developing very strong friendships.

Friendships are spiritual and transcend policy and procedure. For many, friendships seem to intensify during downsizing.

If your friend experiences pain, so do you. If you don't, you are probably strong acquaintances.

"Beloved" is an appropriate word to use when describing meaningful relationships at work.

# Boxes at Work

## *Choices*

- Read *Silent Sabotage: Rescuing Our Careers, Our Companies, and Our Lives From the Creeping Paralysis of Anger and Bitterness* by William J. Morin.
- If you have never been laid off, interview someone who has. See if you can empathize, not just sympathize, but truly experience the same feelings of the laid off person.
- If you have been laid off, or if you are unemployed, seek career counseling if it hasn't been made available to you. It will be worth it.
- If a friend has lost a job recently, the first thing to do is acknowledge his or her loss and the associated feelings. Simply saying "I imagine this must be real painful" will help far more than trying to use logic, such as, "Hang in there, this can't last forever."
- We all yearn to feel deeply understood. It starts with listening, not lecturing—try it with a friend who has lost a job.
- Logic can be highly useful after the initial emotional response to the loss has been experienced and dealt with.

**If you want to develop a shared sense of direction and purpose between the individual and the organization, recognize that it is human nature to see the world differently, and in most cases what I see is not necessarily what you see.**

*—Michael J. Vandermark*

# On the Integration of Personal and Organizational Vision

You are
the asphalt
parking lot

I am
the gum wrapper
in the breeze

We touch
sometimes

# On the Integration of Personal and Organizational Vision

## *Insights*

Totally shared vision of hundreds or thousands of people is a myth.

If our perceptions and realities are different, how can we share the same vision?

Hundreds or thousands of visions of separate individuals woven together in a very loose manner is probably more realistic. Big difference.

Can you recite your organization's mission statement? Vision statement? What is one of your firm's long-term strategic goals?

Who is your company's Chief Operating Officer? How much money is your organization attempting to earn this year?

If your deep-down answer is "don't know" or "not too interested," how can shared vision exist?

# On the Integration of Personal and Organizational Vision

## *Choices*

- An effective way to think of organizational and personal vision is to imagine a large herd of cattle "heading roughly west." Decide if "west" is the way for you.
- Decide what you want out of a career, then find a place that needs what you have to offer.
- That is, match your vision to theirs. It probably won't be a 100% fit, but it will be better than staying where you are, especially if you want to go "east" and they are going "west."
- If you really don't care too much about having a fulfilling job and just anything will do, pay attention to your low energy about fulfillment in life. Focus on your spiritual development. You may have a pleasant surprise coming your way.
- Discuss your organization's mission statement at a staff meeting or another gathering. Facilitate a discussion about alignment of personal and organizational vision.
- If you haven't already, identify your roles and goals for your personal, professional, family, and spiritual life.

**Work is for man and not man for work.**

*—Pope Paul II*

## Majesty Elusive

What creative life force
    runs through these buildings
    tickles meetings
dances in our corporate lives
appears on computer screens
    teases our teams
and so powerfully
affects
our buyers?

This energy, this
sorrowsweet aroma
    of work,
    of passion.
What is its essence,
where is its
core?

I notice timeless moments
and deja vu feelings of contentment.
    Where in my body do
        my feelings originate?
Who is doing
this?
What tactic is in place?

How do I understand?
    Plot? Predict?
        and finalize the action item of passion,
desire, love of work, of contribution, of self,
    of me . . . and you?

I long to capture the majesty
    of this place, weekend sleepy, yet daily alive
        and thunder-driven as a cold wet rain on a
parched desert floor.

This elusive majesty
invades my consciousness suddenly,
and then gone, in the
    voice mail flicker of
        the moment,

            what love is this?

# Majesty Elusive

## *Insights*

The spirit, positive energy, and creativity of the individuals of Corporate America have led to awe-inspiring contributions to mankind.

God is alive and well at work.

Your love of what you do, how you contribute, is manifest in your spiritual development.

Passion in the workplace is like kissing as a teenager—unlimited energy and enjoyment, hoping it lasts forever.

# Majesty Elusive

## *Choices*

- Write ten activities of your job that you love and why you love them.
- Think of ways to improve your performance by finding a way to do more with the activities you identified above.
- Write a proposal to your boss to implement the changes you have thought about. In your proposal, point out how your organization will benefit by allowing the shift to occur.
- Ask a friend to role play with you and practice the actual conversation you will have with your boss.
- In a special meeting with your boss, propose the changes. Soon afterwards, celebrate your courage regardless of the outcome.

**These then are my last words to you: Be not afraid of life. Believe that life is worth living, and your belief will help create the fact.**

*—William James*

# Gather Me

Gather on a hill
a way to remember
people's names . . .
A certain way, hot and
spicy, and systematic. Oh
gather me, still hot and
still spicy, with my agenda

Oh gather me, an employee's
need of sleep, of love,
of spirit, and of an
awareness of my
vulnerability, so I can,
without meaningless long
hours, without results,
learn how to
run a meeting well, and

if need be
to find another job. Why
embrace effort? Why write
down my ideas? The Wall
Street Journal doesn't have
comics.

# Gather Me

## *Insights*

Full-page color comics fit in the Wall Street Journal
about as well as you do in a
job that “isn’t you.”

If you don’t love your job, the “not loving it”
is a signal from your spirit to your intellect. The trick is to use
your intellect to get what your spirit (heart) wants. Do that, and
you’ll be happy with your job . . . guaranteed.

Sometimes work in Corporate America seems like a struggle.

Beneath the struggle, beneath it all, is our constant striving for
meaning in life, even in the face of tasks
we don’t necessarily enjoy.

For many, the workplace is gloomy, depressing, tiring, and
without spiritual reward. If you feel this way,
see the first insight again.

# Gather Me

## *Choices*

- Re-read the Choices section from the poem *Majesty Elusive*. If you notice that you have no energy and feel no excitement about proposing changes to your job, that is an important signal from your spirit.

- Begin a 7-day journaling exercise. Start by committing to writing for 20 minutes, non-stop, every day for 7 consecutive days.

- What to write about? Start by writing about the ideal job for you or your dissatisfaction with the one you have. Don't worry too much about **planning** your writing, just let your thoughts and feelings be identified on paper.

- Another way to get started—write the job you would enjoy if you won the lottery and decided to continue working anyway.

- Shortly after you finish writing, openly discuss your journal entries with a close friend or counselor. Ask for comments about what they notice about you as you describe your writing. Pay attention to what they say.

**Discover your divinity, find your unique talent, serve humanity with it, and you can generate all the wealth that you want. When your creative expressions match the needs of your fellow humans, then wealth will spontaneously flow from the unmanifest to the manifest, from the realm of the spirit to the world of form. You will begin to experience your life as a miraculous expression of divinity—not just occasionally, but all the time. And you will know true joy and the true meaning of success—the ecstasy and exultation of your own spirit.**

*—Deepak Chopra, M.D.*

# Some Definitions

**job description (def)**: a box to fit into.

**paycheck (def)**: a reward for fitting in a box.

**dharma (def)**: purpose in life, fitting comfortably into a box, loving it.

**mission in life (def)**: search for, discover, create dharma.

**fear (def)**: anticipation of danger; loss of courage.

**courage (def)**: the firmness of spirit that faces danger or extreme difficulty without flinching or retreating.

How will your spirit know
bliss at work?
Are you unwilling to seek
your purpose?

Rise. Move about.
Begin.
Movement wakes us up and
unlocks new gifts.

# Some Definitions

## *Insights*

Fear debilitates.

The reason most people stay in jobs they don't enjoy is fear. Period.

Lack of confidence, worry, and fear are obstacles. They are imagined, and represent 90% of the blockages to you getting what you want.

Courage is available to everyone.

You cannot make a wrong decision about improving your job situation. The key is to commit and act on whatever decision you make.

# Some Definitions

## *Choices*

- If you are unhappy at work, write 10 reasons why you should look elsewhere. This writing may help you get in touch with your frustration, disappointment, or anger about your current job, or your excitement about other possibilities.
- Now, write 10 reasons why you wouldn't quit next Friday.
- Chances are, if you are unhappy but won't quit, most of the reasons for staying are driven by some sort of fear.
- Talk about your fear with a person who understands you and is a good listener. Become friends with your fear, that is, the better you understand your scared self, the better **you** will deal with **you**.
- It's all about you. This is good news because of all the people you could try to change, you will have the most luck with you. If you have children, or have ever been one, you know what this means.

**Every scarecrow has a secret ambition to terrorize.**

*—Stansilaus J. Lec*

# Q and A

**Boss**: Am I a good boss?

**Subordinate**: All these years I've attended your staff meetings, worn the T-shirts you ordered, organized the holiday party, traveled when you needed me to, sacrificed vacation time to complete projects, and avoided dating my co-workers.

**Boss**: But, am I a good boss?

**Subordinate**: Are you a good boss? All these years I have never complained about jet lag, avoided being confrontational, worn the right clothes, didn't ask for raises, accepted my performance appraisal as is, never cheated on expense reports, and contained my fear, uncertainty, and doubt.

**Boss**: Then, you feel I am a good boss?

**Subordinate**: Well, of course.

Why is not my heart soothed
by your words, my satisfaction true?
Why this bittersweet attraction
to success and control?

Insecurity runs icy-hot through

the veins of my career
matched only by the burning
authenticity of my fear
always a paradox
deeply rooted, ever attending

Who am I?
And why do I need to
control you?

# Q and A

## *Insights*

Better to have a boss who is like a mentor, a guide, a coach, one who is continually contributing to your learning, than one who micro-manages you.

Micro-management occurs when your boss has to know everything you (and others) do and approve things that don't need a boss's approval.

Micro-managers are driven by
(you guessed it)
fear.

What are they afraid of? Losing control over you. If you don't do what you are supposed to, ultimately they get in trouble.

Luke Skywalker had mentors in the Star Wars Trilogy. Darth Vader wasn't one of them.

# Q and A

## *Choices*

- Ask your boss to be your mentor. Maybe it will work. Be clear about what you want to learn from your boss. State it during your request.
- Be a mentor to someone who works for you. Try acting as if you were their personal consultant rather than one who is there to approve all they do.
- If you feel micro-managed, approach your boss and discuss the issue. Ask for mentorship and guidance (see first insight) and avoid blaming.
- If you are a manager and are interested in ways to increase your effectiveness, read *The Empowered Manager* by Peter Block.
- Urge those in your immediate work area to discuss ways to increase contribution by reassigning job tasks. Align natural talent with real jobs. Except as required by law, eliminate job descriptions, replace them with renegotiated roles and responsibilities.

**The right to be heard does not automatically include the right to be taken seriously.**

*—Hubert Humphrey*

# Real Power

No delayed alibis
now machine
The proper hot

buttons have been
pressed, all is in
order

Procedure has been
followed. This could
mean your job; you're

powerless compared
to me. So, no more games
just give me the fax.

# Real Power

## *Insights*

More machines are doing more "hands-on" work previously accomplished by people. For example, using fax machines eliminates the need for mail delivery.

People are doing more "knowledge" work.

The demand for knowledge is showing up in Corporate America by way of higher educational requirements and expectations.

Bachelor's degrees and graduate degrees are available more and more through quality institutions offering evening or weekend classes or distance learning programs.

Adults of all ages, up into their 60's and 70's (even further), are returning to school. Someone once said to me, "If I go back to school now, I'll be 52 when I finish."
I replied, "You are going to be 52 anyway."

# Real Power

## *Choices*

- Become friends with technology, it is here to stay.
- If the idea of advancing your education appeals to you, call colleges and universities in your area and discover what they have to offer.
- Also, go to your public library, ask the reference librarian to show you the literature describing distance learning programs from universities and institutes throughout the U.S.
- Check out some of the technical trade schools in your area if the notion of returning to school doesn't appeal to you.

**To be what we are, and to become what we are capable of becoming, is the only end in life.**

*—Robert Louis Stevenson*

**Every calling is great when greatly pursued.**

*—Oliver Wendell Holmes, Jr.*

# Worklove

When worklove comes
back into my life
even if I've been
without it for years
I will see how, at
the end of my life,
with just a few breaths
left, it will be easy
for me to speak with
energy and enthusiasm
about life.

# Worklove

## *Insights*

Work requires energy.

Energy stems from desire.

Desire is found in the spirit.

Spirit is found in your heart.

Pay attention to your heart.

# Worklove

## *Choices*

- Interview a person who **truly loves** his or her work. Ask the following questions:
- What led you to choose this work?
- What do you like about it the most?
- What do you like about it the least?
- Is this work spiritual to you?
- What recommendations do you have for people who want spiritual meaning in the work they choose?

**Security is mostly a superstition. It does not exist in nature . . . . Life is either a daring adventure or nothing.**

*—Helen Keller*

# Personal Tactics 1.1.2

maybe we could get in the
flow seek rotational assignments
and develop a life story
own stock in the company

always uphill always
worry over TQM buzzwords and
the real meaning of value

maybe we should take up the cloth
and glance toward anyone who
passes our door
go for the going
tell people who say we aren't
strategic to go to hell

maybe we'll destroy each other
slay dragons everywhere and
let our vacation time expire
my daddy always told me that if

you know your boss wears a hairpiece
surrender and keep the daylight
on the other side of tomorrow
because if you don't it will
come to meet you

# Personal Tactics 1.1.2

## *Insights*

Sometimes we just don't know what we want.

Confusion leads to lack of clarity and causes "stuckness."

Sometimes it's more comfortable to feel
stuck than to face the challenges
and feelings of change.

The whole thing is paradoxical and circular:
Feeling stuck leads to
thinking about change.
Thinking about change leads to
a desire to act.
A desire to act leads to
thinking about acting.
Thinking about acting leads to
reasons why not to act.
Reasons why not to act lead to
feeling stuck. (back to the beginning)

The paradox above is in your **imagination**.
Your opportunities lie in your acting.
Do it.

# Personal Tactics 1.1.2

## *Choices*

- If you are feeling stuck, gather all the courage you can, put your inhibitions at bay for a while, and complete the following exercise:
- Imagine that within you is the "stuck" self as well as the "ready to act" self.
- Assume the voice of your "stuck" self and talk **out loud** to your "ready to act" self as if he or she was sitting in a chair facing you. Say out loud all the reasons for staying stuck. Be emphatic and overemotional.
- After you have mentioned some of the reasons, change to your "ready to act" self and move into the physical place opposite you—the space where you were your "stuck" self. Argue with the "stuck" self from the perspective of the "ready to act" self.
- Continue this dialogue. Watch for some insights about the inner conflict you are experiencing between the you that is ready to act and the you that is stuck.
- If the exercise above seems silly or if it doesn't do much, find a counselor to help.

**I'm caught in a power struggle. My boss has the power, and I have the struggle.**

*—Bill Halliburton*

# Sort Of

**Per your request, enclosed please find**

cubicle sounds of
harsh reality and
staples stacks of
wilted faith, readily,
cheerfully, accepting
practiced autocracy

**It has come to our attention that**

impassioned spirits calm
pain and chaos, love
dissipates tyranny
and hope tickles
the underbelly of
passion, and

**If you need assistance or additional information, please contact**

our company bishops and cardinals
that give us our daily bread, ask
for the person in charge, be ready
for force and conflict, and
remember, no matter what,

the empowered employees make
the decisions around here

Sort of.

# Sort Of

## *Insights*

Empowerment works . . . sometimes.

The question is not "How to empower?"
The question is "Why empower?"

Many organizations try to mandate empowerment without understanding the structural and systemic changes needed first.

If your boss understands how empowerment works, and if you want power, it works.

If you don't really want power and/or your boss doesn't know how to give it to you, it doesn't work.

Empowering others is a learned competency that leads to tremendous results in organizations that have invested time and energy, as well as money, learning how to do it.

# Sort Of

## *Choices*

- If the idea of empowerment appeals to you, whether you are a manager or not, browse through any of the increasing number of books on the topic. They are in the business section of the bookstore.
- Make a list of reasons why you **want** more power at work.
- Make a list of reasons why you **need** more power at work.
- Compare the lists, talk about them with a soulmate at work. If you don't have a soulmate at work, a very close friend will do.
- Empowerment lends itself nicely to being proactive. It starts by you acting on your own, taking risks, to serve a higher purpose or entity. The power rests in you. Its keeper is your spirit. Act on it.

**The "reality" that is left behind in any ending is not just a picture on the wall. It is a sense of which way is up and which way is down; it is a sense of which way is forward and which way is backward. It is, in short, a way of orienting oneself and moving forward into the future.**

*—William Bridges*

# Rightsizing John and Mary

See John run.
See Mary fall.
Tension thick
the air like the
leftover smell
of strategy, downsizing, and
midsummernight's dreams of
upwardly mobile
bottom lines.

See Mary run.
See John fall.
Boxes of fear exiting
after hours,
scrutiny close, watching
from empty survivor eyes . . .
wondering.

Spirits drained,
longing laid off,
meaning held hostage
like dead leaves on a
live oak tree, waiting . . .

Emptiness thoughts
caress the essence of

life and work, family and home,
children's hopes,
while bottomline
tactics breathe new expectations into
lost times gone by,
each giving, somehow, the
appearance of the other.

To your eyes now,
what looks like water
burns, what looks like fire
is a great relief to be on
the inside. In the aftermath,
God's tricks are amazing,
but for the sake of conversation,
there is your story to
tell. Where are your
friends?

See John and Mary run and fall.

# Rightsizing John and Mary

## *Insights*

There is a predictable drop in morale, productivity, and commitment following layoffs.

Trust in management plummets, loyalty decreases significantly, corporate theft increases, the grapevine rages, and people spend more time wondering who's next.

Typical feelings in a "right-sized" company include fear, anxiety, anger, disappointment, sadness, bewilderment, exhaustion, and many similar negative emotions.

One well-respected Chief Executive Officer developed a formula: 1/2 x 2 x 3—He wants half the number of employees doing twice the amount of work, and getting three times the productivity.

This can work **if** (big if) the spirit is engaged and Dharma is created.

# Rightsizing John and Mary

## *Choices*

- Dharma is word from Eastern cultures related to finding purpose in life. To decrease your chances of being laid off, try this: discover your purpose, make the necessary changes, and seek Dharma. Organizations recognize people who are in love with their work and who are good at it. They seem to survive layoffs.
- Even if you are not in the job market, update your resume now!
- Update your resume by asking yourself these questions:

**What is it I actually do?**

**How will someone know I've done it?**

**If I wasn't at work "doing it," what would happen?**

- Stay ahead of your job search by identifying a network of contacts. Start with family and close friends, move out into the community from there. Be sure your network knows exactly what you want, how else can they help you?

**The world is full of lonely people, each isolated in a private, secret dungeon.**

*—Loretta Girzartis*

# Electronic Affair

Voice mail
    from you
    is so like
cold, harsh
    truth.

Who cares?
    Not me
    remember
I said
    no.

The way
    you left
    your message
left me
    so

shut down,
    inane.
    I wanted
to be
    free,

but there
    was work

to be done.
You win.
Now

it's time
that you
discover
about
love,

and me,
that I
never was
really
drawn

to your
voice mail
messages
anyway.

The most
I got
from you was
your busy
signal.

# Electronic Affair

## *Insights*

People who work well together often share common interests and/or a common purpose.

Sharing a common purpose or common interests is usually a prerequisite for developing friendship.

Combine friendship at work with physical attraction . . . BINGO!

Romance occurs in Corporate America.

Irony: **love** is what Corporate America needs and longs for (it is called morale), yet romance at work is "against policy" in many organizations.

# Electronic Affair

## *Choices*

- If you find yourself attracted to another human being at work or otherwise, that is you sending a message to you. . . it's spiritual. You cannot find the source of your attraction in your physical body, it simply isn't there.
- Pay attention to how you choose to respond to the message.
- Journaling works well here. Keep a daily record of what you notice about your feelings, attitude, and behavior toward the other person. See what happens.
- One way to handle attraction is to be straightforward with the one you are attracted to. Tell the person about your attraction if you feel comfortable doing so. Think twice if he or she is your boss.
- Why? Even though you may feel OK with disclosing your feelings, your boss may not. This is tricky, and political. Be careful.

**We trust, sir, that God is on our side. It is more important to know that we are on God's side.**

*—Abraham Lincoln*

# Risk Taking

Move your corporate vision
ahead strongly, the way
will spring open to you.

Become bankrupt and destroyed,
you will be flooded
with aliveness.

Hold to corporate citizenship,
humble your organization among others,
you will grow stronger than the strongest.

Your spirit will become
known to you, without
you.

# Risk Taking

## *Insights*

Chaos and crisis create growth.

Growth means coming together with focus, direction, and energy and then acting on it.

Failures are gifts.

Contributing to others
ultimately leads to you receiving from others.

The type of contribution referred to above is sometimes called
corporate citizenship.

# Risk Taking

## *Choices*

- Discuss your firm's vision and values among friends at work. Does your vision include serving the community in some fashion?
- If your company has a voluntary program or another way to serve the community, get involved. You will be rewarded.
- If your company doesn't have a program of community service, ask around. Start one. Check out other organizations that have programs in place.
- Have there been times in the past when your organization was in serious financial trouble? What happened that enabled recovery? What was spiritual (morale-driven) about the recovery?
- Tell the story. Often.

**Choose a job you love, and you will never have to work a day in your life.**

*—Confucius*

**Everyone has a purpose in life . . . . a unique gift or special talent to give to others. And when we blend this unique talent with service to others, we experience the ecstasy and exultation over our own spirit, which is the ultimate goal of all goals.**

*—Deepak Chopra, M.D.*

# Alive

Longing for workmeaning
    arouses a passion in me

Let the world be my torturer
    not you, passion

Don't kick me
    when I'm down

Don't annihilate the one you
    have made, for the first time, alive

# Alive

## *Insights*

Loving your work is a gift.

Better to deal with extra problems
in your life than to lose passion
for what you do.

Sometimes we feel kicked by life.
Guess who's doing the kicking?

The kicking comes from the self-image.
Who gets kicked? Your heart.

Ouch.

# Alive

## *Choices*

- Discover workmeaning. Create Dharma.
- Right now, in this moment, decide if you want to take steps toward a more meaningful career.
- If you decided to take steps forward, write what they are. Use a career counselor if you are not certain about how to start. Re-read this book for hints.
- If you are fulfilled, congratulate yourself.
- If you decided not to move forward because you don't have the energy or because you are undecided, write a brief letter to yourself and list 3 reasons why.
- Turning this page and leaving the issue unaddressed is a signal from your intellect to your spirit.

**The task ahead of us is never as great as the power behind us.**

*—Ralph Waldo Emerson*

# Who's In Charge Here?

I reach for an idea. It
turns into strategy.
Coincidence?

I do some listening. It
turns out meaningfully, souls
respond.

I say one must not travel, instead
save and prosper . . .
it works!

On the way to the workplace
I notice unexpected good
simply . . . is.
I wonder . . . who's **really**
running the place?

Coincidence?

# Who's in Charge Here?

## *Insights*

The source of all creation, including ideas and strategies,
is located in the spiritual realm.

The deepest hunger of the human soul is
to be listened to intently
and to be understood.

It **is** possible to create a dynamic, energetic,
profitable, high-spirited workforce.

Creating such an outcome begins with awareness
of self, especially for people who have power and influence.

Organizations often take on the personality
and attitudes of the leader.

# Who's in Charge Here?

## *Choices*

- Pray for your organization, however large or small. May seem unusual, but it works.
- Compliment someone during the next hour. Anyone, any compliment.
- Offer a sign of appreciation to someone who helps you in some way. Greeting cards are wonderful, so are flowers (even just one), and small tokens of appreciation.
- Even though you might not believe it, most men enjoy receiving flowers. Try it, you may be surprised.
- Give your **self** (spirit) a gift, a thank you for all your hard work. Treat yourself to a ritual or celebration centered on your contributions at work.
- Try a bubble bath with candlelight and soft music. Take a moment to appreciate you, your spirit at work. Then enjoy.

**What you value is what you think about. What you think about is what you become.**

*—Joe Weldon*

# Shoes

Your anxiety over your business
trip dulls the patent leather
read-their-minds glistening,
leaping hysterically from "proper" ness
emblazoned on your
shoes.

Suppose you lose track of
what you do, drift from
tactics to heart, to intuitive
self, to soul? Will someone
really ask? And if so,
can you defeat them, acclaim
victory?

Rumor has it . . . that
shoes in proper shape always
win, but the real question is:

What will be spoken
    about you at your
        funeral?

# Shoes

## *Insights*

In Corporate America, it's easy to focus
on "beating the competition."

The competition is made up
of people.

For some, competing and winning means pulverizing people,
defeating their spirit, annihilating them.

Sometimes we find ourselves holding to personal
values that are negative and destructive.

Who among your friends, family, and acquaintances
would avoid attending your funeral?

Why?

# Shoes

## *Choices*

- Imagine you are attending your own funeral. Picture the event vividly in your imagination, then answer the following questions. Discuss your answers with a soulmate.
- What would a speaker from your family have to say about you?
- What would a speaker from your church, synagogue, or other place of worship have to say about you?
- What would someone from your place of work have to say about you?
- What would the people you compete with have to say about you?
- What would you have to say about you?

**Be willing to speak of traditional religion, no matter how offended some group members may be. Overcome the bias against the word God. The great force of our spiritual roots lies in tradition, like it or not.**

**The wise leader models spiritual behavior and lives in harmony with spiritual values. There is a way of knowing, higher than reason; there is a self, greater than egocentricity.**

—*John Heider*

# Self-Knowledge

Vacant heartsounds pound for
fulfillment
eliminate the torture
of **intellectually** (only) knowing
leadership and spirit

Cross the boundary between
technology and love
soul and blueprint
heart and strategy

Secrets untold lie
in the beauty of
knowing self
Not holiness shows
or material success but
center-of-your-chest
delight that mercilessly unfolds
awakening your spiritual fire

If you want to know the
SOURCE
if you want to know the
ONE

hold yourself to
yourself

# Self-Knowledge

## *Insights*

Understanding theories of leadership is one thing, acting as a good leader is another.

It is scary to talk about spirituality in the workplace, at least for many people.

The gift in life is to know your innermost being, your spiritual fire.

If your higher power, God, is in you, then it follows that knowing yourself well helps you to know God better. "Hold yourself to yourself" means paying attention to your spirit.

Spiritual awareness often leads to material success, not the other way around.

# Self-Knowledge

## *Choices*

- Find a spiritual guide.
- Start down the path.
- Learn meditation, prayer, introspection, and just being quiet.
- Take good care of your body. You live in it. If you wreck it, where are you going to live?
- If you lead others, seek feedback about your effectiveness. If you want to know about the spirituality of your workplace, ask about morale. You will get some formidable clues that way.

**It's OK to feel anything. You may feel griefstricken, angry, like a failure, exhausted, muddled, lost, beaten, indecisive, relieved, overwhelmed, inferior, melancholy, giddy, silly, loathful, full of self-hatred, envious, suicidal, disgusted, happy, outraged, in rage, or anything else.**

*—Melba Colgrove*
*—Harold Bloomfield*
*—Peter McWilliams*

# Phlegm

The man had womanly eyes
after grief, molested by
uncertainty. And there was
the way he sat,
unattended attention.

He looked not quite young, tanned,
very board room, very achieving,
self-achieving.
He took the
papers like junk mail, without
a firmness,
without . . . . . feeling;
no attention, little movement. Otherwise
he sat blankly
gazing past years of inhaling the
spirit of this workplace. Past
compatibility and compassionability, he looked
directly and coldly, and with
overbalance, sternly, unknowingly
into my eyes.

The corpse of his livelihood strewn like
death ashes,
broken notions of security,

peace, comfort, and knowing,
he came to the meeting as if he had been
glued to his death.

A dim, gray thickness hung in the space, an
alive thickness
that he drew silently in with each
calculated breath.
Through lips and nostrils, down
his throat he swallowed
the message reluctantly like reswallowing
chest cough phlegm
longing for expulsion, for freedom. Words that
stuck in his throat, and
in his heart, words that sifted
through his ideas of predictability and security
and peace.

And with a devastating almost silence, and in
five words, and five
only,
he questioned

My position has been eliminated?

# Phlegm

## *Insights*

Reswallowing chest cough phlegm is disgusting.
So is having your position eliminated.

Grief and uncertainty can be highly immobilizing.

For many people, job loss is
one of the greatest ongoing fears of their lives.

Although most people are shaken severely by unexpected
job loss, nearly 90% of those people report later on
in life that the loss was one of the best
things that ever happened to them.

A majority of people who have been laid off
report finding a job that pays more
and is more satisfying.

# Phlegm

## *Choices*

- Update your resume, keep it updated.
- Adopt a healthy attitude recognizing you could lose your job, or your business **could** fail.
- Knowing your job is never completely secure keeps you alert to other possibilities. Stay in touch with your network of friends and business acquaintances.
- If you lost your job today (anything is possible), what would you do? How would you feel? Talk about this with someone you care about and who cares about you.
- Go to the library or bookstore. Look through some of the books on career development. Don't look for anything specific, just browse. Notice how you feel about being there, looking.
- What you notice about how you feel is another signal from your spirit.

**Every man shall receive his own reward according to his own labor.**

*—I Corinthians*

# In Defense of Bottom Lines

"Herb worries too much
about the dumb bottom line"
according to Geraldine. She says
job satisfaction is a fantasy and that
you can never make friends at work anyway;
that you have to be at home to have fun,
and that a job is just a job. She says,
"No one here cares about the people,
they never tell us anything."

Geraldine really wants a covered parking space
but says "only mucky mucks get 'em,
cause they know somebody."
Sometimes Geraldine laughs real hard
when her boss makes a mistake and
sometimes she says "It's not my job."

Geraldine says she always buys
best-you-can-get clothes, and
her car is shiny and new. She says
she likes living alone so she can
fix her place up the way **she** wants it.

Geraldine says she's been here
a long, long time and

she has all the money she needs for
retirement and she likes to count it,
especially when she is on vacation.

Geraldine says
"I'll be happy when I'm out of here,
what did they ever do for me
anyway?"

That's what Geraldine says.

# In Defense of Bottom Lines

## *Insights*

The bottom line is crucial, not dumb.

Healthy bottom lines relate to you receiving a paycheck.

We all love paychecks.

A bureaucracy is a class system, that is, different classes of people are identified within the system.

Bureaucracies create opportunities to have mucky-mucks.

Some people dislike being in the "lower class."

Geraldine is one of them.

# In Defense of Bottom Lines

## *Choices*

- Sit comfortably, decide to be honest and straightforward with yourself, and answer this question: "How do I **really** feel about people who work with me and who have more power and privilege than me?"

- If you have spent much time in Corporate America, you have been exposed to the notion that moving up and obtaining more power and privilege is a natural desire, that is, you <u>should</u> want it. This is self-image stuff.

- Problem is . . . what happens if you don't get it? Discuss your answer with a good friend or soulmate.

- Good news. We are all equal spiritually.

**One of the main factors differentiating humans from other animals is the awareness of self: the ability to form an identity and then attach a value to it. In other words, you have the capacity to define who you are and then decide if you like that identity or not.**

*—Matthew McKay*
*—Patrick Fanning*

# What Do You Want From Me?

Interest in you?
A tug on your ego?
Love of your idea?

This is the fabric of
Corporate America
Don't say
"Take care of me"
Instead
Breathe your inner music
Dance your dance

Listen to the inside of
what you say

I am you
looking back
at
you

# What Do You Want From Me?

## *Insights*

We all want recognition, appreciation, and love in
our lives, especially at work. Most of us spend more time at
work than anywhere else. Count the hours.

Sometimes we depend so much on others to deliver
what we need, we lose contact with
our spiritual center.

Corporate America is a playground of opportunity,
overflowing with all sorts of recognition and
appreciation; however, it all starts
with you appreciating you.

If the notion of "you appreciating you" or
"I am you looking back at you" is meaningless or
confusing, that is another signal from
your spirit to your intellect.

Acting on the signal is
healthy and will
move you forward on your spiritual path.

# What Do You Want From Me?

## *Choices*

- Breathe your inner music, dance your inner dance. That is, do what you are here to do.
- If you are unclear about what you are here to do, find a helper. Get the answer. It's worth it.
- Pay attention to the inside of what you say, your feelings. Your body sends you messages about whether you are in balance or not. Ulcers, high blood pressure, heart disease, even cancer have been linked to the mind/body connection.
- Life is both a serious and fun journey. Corporate America offers the opportunity to have fun and be serious. Be both.
- Maybe someday wildflowers will grow on Wall Street.

## *Twelve Signs of Inner Peace*

Loss of interest in conflict

Frequent attacks of smiling

Frequent overwhelming attacks of appreciation

Loss of desire to judge ourselves

Loss of interest in judging others

Unmistakable ability to enjoy each moment

Tendency to think and act spontaneously rather than from
fear based on past experience

Loss of interest in interpreting the actions of others

Loss of the ability to worry (a serious symptom)

Contented feelings of connectedness to others and nature

Increasing susceptibility to love extended by others
as well as an uncontrollable urge to extend it

Increasing tendency to let things happen
rather than make things happen

—Author Unknown

# *Index*

Dr. Vandermark is available for speeches, presentations, workshops and consulting in areas related to this book. For further information, please call **Spirit-at-Work Publications** at 1-602-266-2468, or write to 1459 E. McLellan Boulevard, Phoenix, Arizona 85014.